Time is a Snake's Tongue

Time is a Snake's Tongue

Poems

MaryAnn L. Miller

CW Books

© 2023 MaryAnn L. Miller

Published by CW Books
P.O. Box 541106
Cincinnati, OH 45254-1106

ISBN: 978-1-62549-437-5

Poetry Editor: Kevin Walzer
Business Editor: Lori Jareo

Visit us on the web at www.readcwbooks.com

Table of Contents

Studio Trees..7
Ormolu Clock at the Rosenbach Museum Philadelphia............8
Anywhere Birds Meet is a Church...................................9
Dinner Theater..10
Snake Path 11
My Armor Is Silence...12
A Debt to Mrs. Barnhart..13
Our Town..14
When Music Stops..15
Trans-specied 16
Sam Mohawk..18
A conversation with my brother that started with Doggy
    Cavaliero...19
The Air Raid Warden 20
Ronnie..21
Catholic Race Theory 22
Classroom Discussion Catholic School in the Fifties.................23
Remembering the Great Migratory Trail........................24
Red Tail..25
From my son when I asked about his First Memory
    of Racism..26
From my daughter when I asked about her First Memory
    of Racism..27
How Anxiety Works..28
Night Time Mind..29
Racism Changes at the Speed of Aging.........................30
Harbingers..31
Questions for the Defendant (Accusations)...................32
Art in the Time of Savages 33
Would you die for your faith?......................................34
In the Cradle of Liberty 35
Autopsy for a Martyr..36
My Horse Blueway...37
Immutable..38

Acknowledgments..41
About the Author...43

Studio Trees

In my studio, trees grow
made of paper and ink.
The paper is smooth
on one side rough on the other,
the ink a chemical
burn forced through

the screen.
See the skulls that
appear among the leaves.
It could be a bouquet
of dried white magnolias.
But, it's a copse

of ink trees, hiding
history. When it snows
the skulls disappear
forget about them,
life is beautiful,
peaceful again.

Don't part the leaves
or shake the snow
down, you would see
the Black corpses
hanging there still
waiting for justice.

Ormolu Clock at the Rosenbach Museum Philadelphia

Two delicate serpents holding
our diminishments on a Baillon clock.
Time is a snake's tongue flicking at
the hours, the other clicking off minutes.

The circle of time spins slowly
swelling thoughts of the past
mashing them into the present
with shocking naiveté.

Truth comes out.
Omissions cause questions
or repressions. A golden clock
cannot camouflage the ugliness of history.

Seconds tick by and fly into each other;
people live within those seconds
dark nights of collisions
between memory and what has become.

This clock has been gagged.
What has not been counted?
Gone by unmarked, leaving
gilt and craft to museum eternity

an exquisite creation, with no function.
Our bodies, not timeless, full of guilt
and guile wear from the inside like
gold pounded into powder.

Anywhere Birds Meet is a Church

1964 Fourth of July parade in this white New Jersey town
marching band from Malcolm X Shabazz High School in Newark.
That cadence penetrated our diaphragms
resounded in our bone skulls
shook the legs of the old half-dead neighbors.

Those high school kids had feathers on their heads
round hats with plumes bobbing as they strutted their stuff
down Center Street right past my rental house
lighting up that asphalt with shiny blaring brass,
infectious beat ricocheting off tuned snare drums.

Anywhere birds meet is a church,
bringing ancestors with them.

Dinner Theater
After Cornelius Eady

Feathered hats kept in round boxes
reserved for Sunday worship and dinner
theater matinees at noon, bus rides
from Newark to suburbia, where I
waitress so my children will have Christmas.

Women their crests perched on proud heads
recently bowed in prayer, feet twitching,
anticipating, on the bus for an hour,
matching dresses with jackets with chapeaux
conversation like music contralto sopranos.

Laughter rising up that high roof decorated
like a cathedral with pine bough swags.
Table-hopping gold finches, scarlet cardinals,
passerine perchers sashaying, exchanging
pointed pleasantries, Ysatis perfumed hugs.

On the Program: Amahl and the Night Visitors
sung by New York talent–
Does it compare to the music they've already heard this morning?
Aretha Franklin will sing in her inauguration hat in a future
none of us can see clearly in the barely parting snow.

Snake Path

I learned about racism at my grandmother's house. I didn't know what to call it except meanness. Sonny Barnhart, the only black child on that immigrant block in Lyndora, PA came up the steps into the yard to play with my sister and I. We were about five and three. We played tag around the white hydrangea in the side yard. He chased us and we ran around that bush until we were out of breath. Sonny asked me for a drink of water. I went into the kitchen to get him one, as I was moving the stepstool over so I could reach the glass my grandmother asked me what I was doing. I told her I was getting some water for Sonny.

She said to tell him to go home and drink his own water. I told him what she had said. He said, "Oh, okay." and left. I knew even then that wasn't right. I knew it had something to do with his color. What I didn't realize until much later was no one would drink out of that glass if Sonny used it. Grandma would have to throw it away. There were unspoken boundaries you didn't know
about until you stepped over one, especially for Italian immigrants who had to stay on the good side of white people.

Later, when I was in high school, I overheard a conversation about Sonny being arrested for following a white girl home from school. His house was the last one on the block. That put him in the position of always following someone, unless he waited until everyone had passed him and they were safe in their houses.

My Armor Is Silence

My verbs are wishes.
As long as I'm
quiet I will be okay.
My mouth is shut
but my skin shouts.

A Debt to Mrs. Barnhart

Mrs. Barnhart knew she couldn't go into that
Italian house, nor did she want to deliver this overheard
message. She did it because she knew the right thing was not
to deny someone a job.

It was so unusual for the woman to climb
the stairs from the sidewalk, come onto the porch,
that my mother met her at the door, perhaps thinking
to stop her coming in.

If she had ignored Mrs. Barnhart on the porch rapping
on the summer screen door, if she had peered
around the curtains, seen the colored lady
and hid from her–

If my mother hadn't taken Mrs. Barnhart's advice
and gone to Paganelli's corner store to check on that
phone call, she would have missed getting
her first good job.

How do I think about this gift Mrs. Barnhart gave to my mother?
A gift given with no assurance of gratitude,
how she must have turned it over in her mind.
A debt accrues

over time into un-payable reparations, defeats
are pre-written on immigrant scorecards; slaves
were counted as property in census records. My grandfather
was designated "dark-complected" in his.

My mother could have been served another defeat
never understanding what she did wrong, not good enough,
but for Mrs. Barnhart's generosity of spirit,
how her mother raised her.

Our Town

Our town was made of steel, Armco barriers, and Bantam Jeeps.
Armcos guarded the roads from Pittsburgh to Baltimore.

Kept people on the straight and narrow. The jobs went to the
sons of immigrants from Italy and the Ukraine.

(Imaginary Negroes were just waiting somewhere
to take those jobs from our dads.)

We were granted a kind of upward mobility they could
only dream of in their end of the ghetto street houses.

They didn't have an ice cube's chance in hot tea to move
from the street of the steel mill to a lot in the suburbs.

When Music Stops

When music stops it's like a small death.
After Bob Marley Three Little Birds

Starlings flying into harp strings
wings trapped flapping flashing
in momentary dazzle
caught in a tangle
dissonant vibrating
claws skittering
until they lay still.
Small bodies belly up– water covering
them. No one will find them or know
they ever lived, but the resonance, the energy
of their miniature struggle continues
is released as a vaporous chuckling song
up through the swampy damp.

Trans-specied

What northern tweet accompanied
his fluttering in the cradle, his open mouth
yearning, eyes to the sky?

I sensed
he would not live satisfied
with boy feet.

He was a jumper, then
a leaper, then a pole-vaulter
trying to get more air.

Hawks riding thermals made him shudder.
Visits to the aviary caused
his eyes to thin with plotting.

When he began to shave maps were strewn
on the bathroom floor.
He rode the bus to Newark Liberty.

At nineteen, he bloomed. His shirts could not
contain the wings. His shins curled.
He brought me eggshells and bromeliads

but threw aside the cape I gave him,
exposed his feathered neck,
his wide black span; flew straight up.

Please come back, I begged,
tell me what you like to eat,
I'll make it for you.

From his beaking lips I heard:
rodents, hatchlings,
small bony fish.

Sam Mohawk

Sam Mohawk was originally buried at the corner of Monroe and East Pearl in Butler, PA. He was known as the Indian who massacred six people at the Old Stone House on Route 8 North, in 1840. The reason he killed them was the Wigtons who lived there, had him sign a paper giving them all his land. When he realized what the paper said, he killed them all. The Old Stone House massacre story leaves the impression that a band of Indians attacked the family just because they were there, but my brother told me it was only Sam and he was hung for the crime. Probably Sam Mohawk was not his real name, but a moniker white folks had given him.

This reminded me of another story my father told me. As a child, he was part of a posse that hunted down an Indian (Native) who had taken a white woman as his wife. They caught him and tied him to a stake and proceeded to burn him. My father said the fire went out and all that got burned was his pant legs. They were probably drunk and couldn't set a proper fire. They untied him and let him go home to his wife, whom none of them really knew or cared about anyway.

A conversation with my brother that started with Doggy Cavaliero...

I recalled Doggy as the numbers runner
on the South Side, but my brother said that was
Maggie Gregory in her store on Hickory Street
and the guy who picked up the numbers was
the Tick Tock Bread Man
He allowed that perhaps Doggy did run from store
to store, including Laurent's corner store on South Street
Doggy played Semi-pro Baseball
Used to sunbath in the nude in Center Field
at Pullman Park that Butler High School used as an athletic field
He was the groundskeeper
Doggy was a scout for the NY Yankees
He had a gold card that would get him into
any stadium in the country
Would show it to you if you knew to ask
He was known as the Pullman Park Soldier
and had a Medal of Honor for being at Normandy
He was from Lyndora where my mother grew up
He was always dressed in a baseball uniform at
Pullman Park when there was a game
He scooted never walked
even down the steps into the dugout

Flem Zerellino shot a bear with a shotgun
that had an octagonal barrel. A digression.
But what about Doggy?

Doggy tended bar at the Adrian Club in the Monroe
Hotel on Jefferson Street
The Adrian Club was a club for Italians
They sponsored my brother's Pony League team
There was a barbershop next door. Johnny De Rose was the barber
Mom sent my brother there for his haircuts

The Air Raid Warden

There was another barber closer
to our house on Locust Street
His name was Schaffner
He was an air raid warden during WWII
Italians didn't like him because he reported people
for not closing their curtains
He came to our house and flirted with mom
My five-year-old brother threw his rocking horse at him
hit him in the ankles and told Dad
This is why he had to change barbers

Ronnie

My sister and I used to play with Ronnie Vavro,
he had toys we didn't have:
a play kitchen for play cooking,
and lots of dolls.
Ronnie wanted to be a tata girl   (a drum majorette)
He had a baton that he could twirl,
throwing it up in the air and catching it.
Ronnie became a soldier.
During the Korean War my brother came across
Ronnie at Fort Hood during basic training.
I wonder if he ever twirled his rifle.

Catholic Race Theory

Never heard one.   (a theory)
Assumed there were
no Catholic Negroes.   (It was 1949, I was in Fifth grade)

We did have pagan babies to ransom
with our scrounged-up begged-
from-neighbors pennies slotted
into pasteboard cards. Each slot
was covered with a circle to be
pried up to place the coin inside

           (a printed image of an African
           baby in a diaper was on each circle
           They looked like raisins scattered
           across the card.)

What were we ransoming them from?
Babies unbaptized went to Limbo,
these babies were desperate to be
baptized, be released from Limbo,
and given Biblical names.
They could never be white, but
they could have white
Western Pennsylvania names.

Classroom Discussion Catholic School in the Fifties

If it's between the baby or the mother
the baby gets to live.
(To be counted as Catholic, I supposed.)

Who decides? I asked.
The priest.
(How did he get in the delivery room? I wondered.)

Who takes care of the other children? I asked.
The grandmother.

What if the grandmother died in Italy? I wanted to ask, but didn't.

And, also, what about the father?
He had to go to his job every day, and couldn't be expected to take care of children.

The word abortion was not mentioned.

Remembering the Great Migratory Trail

We seek to escape the false lines and boundaries
drawn by men who attempt to bind and separate.

Gerrymandering won't hold a net full of holes
with connective tissue made of native hope.

Nature is against all that binding and boundary-making
laying out before us expanses of behavior, of journey without

markers without maps. Birds know this. They fly
using interior maps looking down on us, avoiding

nets and shotguns to reach the places they know are safe, locations
where they can nest. This is what nature gives us as rest, as comfort.

Are we not a related species? Survival has become an aspect
of DNA, mutated into chromosomes by centuries of vigilance.

Birds are quick in movement and mutation. Their beaks
change at the crack of a seed, speed of necessity.

Changed diet, changed geography, if your yard
is hatching grubs, starlings will arrive ready to peck.

They'll eat the young salamanders slithering under
leaves composting next to the foundation of houses.

If the place is right, they'll stay and build a nest where you
least expect to find that scavenged, pillowy, temporary home.

Red Tail

April window opens to the Western New Jersey sky
hear that wind-sail wing span
as she glides up on heated thermals
a high altitude screeee– a predatory device
resounding off hills measuring distance with precision.
She soars, dives:

shriek of a rabbit, splurt of fur in the hedge.
That dying cry an echo of predator cry
nailing prey to the ground.
Her beak shredding meat for her nestlings a quarter mile
away in some nameless conifer, expecting death on their behalf.

Every year I look for this early Spring hunt.
After living in the same place for fifty years,
I've learned the bloody battles go on as if my witness
means nothing to these creatures who inhabit the land
longer than I can live on it.

Now someone else thinks they own this hunting field
across the road, will build houses on it. The front-end loaders will
carry away soil to big wheeled trucks, the river a few hundred yards
downhill.
Trenchers dig footings for eighty houses. She will nest out in the
country, compete with eagles on the reservoir, hoping they'll stick to
fish.

After the clacking thumping machines leave, the landscape planted,
she'll come back to kill bunnies in the backyards.

From my son when I asked about his First Memory of Racism

Garret Morris on Saturday Night Live, singing "I'm gonna get me a shotgun and kill all the whities I see!" It was funny and everyone laughed. I remember the Clark Dolls Mr. Demkey told us about in Social Studies Class at North.
Dr. Clark had a white doll and a black doll and he asked white and black children to pick which was the good doll. Even the black children picked the white doll. I'll never forget that.

From my daughter when I asked about her First Memory of Racism

We lived next door to the only black family in town. All the kids called the oldest boy Stymie.
We played together all the time. Especially, Stymie and Stanley, the two boys. The girls were younger. But in school, people would throw pennies in front of the Jewish kids; call Italian kids wops.

How Anxiety Works

Children used to visit their neighbors;
we've lost the folkways.
We are separated by significant white plastic fences.
The community is scattered by proximity

by anxiety, proofed by internet,
that nebulous all-present entity–
a study said that anxious parents
produce aggressive children.

Years ago, the school children
all knew about Chester the Molester,
would warn each other one generation
after another, would fear losing

their freedom to walk home from school,
the best part of the day, jumping cracks,
crunching leaves, snow ball fights,
now they just fear.

Night Time Mind

a witch on
a horse flies across
a blood moon
where is love?
there will be snow
beyond the fence
wake up before
a knife turns
you into a soldier
a scarf covering
half your face

Racism Changes at the Speed of Aging

The thing speaks for itself.
It's taken this long for me to describe
white people by their skin color.

I needed to be old not to care if they
were stirred up. It's surprising how
upset they are to be identified by race.

Italian families were always afraid
of the *throwback* a dark baby suddenly
turning up. First thing my mother said

when she saw my first born was
she's so fair. At the time, I thought
it was an odd comment, but then I realized

how long she must have worried about
that. What a useless waste of energy she
could have put into caring about us.

I know I'm classified as "white" but
I actually am two percent Sub-Saharan–
would have made me black at one time.

I sent my swab to National Geographic.
It was worth the two hundred dollars
to learn that information.

Harbingers

Birds are predictors, their name
says it: *ornis* > omen in Greek.

When dirt diggers notice birds flying in, they get nervous
they see them as omens of what is to come.

Canary in the coal mine an ominous
role of songbirds, their music

stopped a sign of deadly vapors. The yellow bird
lies silent in his cage, time to get out.

Primitive alarm systems are used
to advantage but they have to cage one first

birds don't cooperate with stalkers
who are afraid of being supplanted.

Blanket merchants want more white babies but they have
to trap a woman first, fuck her mind then her body.

Deny her any say in the matter.
What's she going to do? Leave the state?

Give her the honor of going through
broken glass first. See if she gets shot.

Anywhere birds gather is a church but
snakes have burrowed into the foundation.

They'll come right into the Wednesday evening
prayer group to raise their gun-shaped heads.

Questions for the Defendant (Accusations)

When you sought a gun, who was it you planned to shoot?
You have been instructed in scapegoating.
You belong to the militia of mistaken country.
You are the hypnotized, the superior skinned,
the paranoid wary of the wrong things.
You cluck like a chicken in a vaudeville show.

When you got that gun, who was it you planned to shoot?
You must have had someone in mind, that you'd claim
to be afraid of when the mesmerist snapped his fingers;
a literal triggering of your hate glands making venom
spew like bullets screaming from your lungs
firing too many times to be self-defense.

Almost makes me want to buy a gun.
Who is it I plan to shoot?

Art in the Time of Savages

Along the border all drawings have
been taken down not one left

to point a direction for our feet.
We might know the way if we had

wings to spread above the shining
twist of water.

The place of no location has flung
us away from Frida's baby.

Don't come here
lullabies are spiders in the bed.

They plan to rub us out
before we can make frantic art

in a jackal world.
Our scraping must matter

it reverberates like
a green poppy sending smoke.

Would you die for your faith?

During the Cold War, Sister could
ask: *Would you die for your faith?*
If the Communists tortured you
how long would you hold out
before you would deny Christ?

There was always the possibility
of a Russian dungeon.
They might pull out my
fingernails one by one.
Maybe they would wrap barbed

wire around my head– a crown
of thorns. What if I would be
crucified or gassed or burned in an oven
or starved or had my breasts cut off or shot
and thrown in a mass grave.

Maybe I should give up my
faith, become a Communist
they would let me go, and
later, if I survived,
I could go to confession.

In the Cradle of Liberty

I rehearse for the worst—
I conjure scenarios
of defense
against the dense
views of the few
who read my skin ticket
then let me in
or let me go.
I practice the perfect
combinations of words
to conceal the smart-ass woman
lurking behind my eyes,
I'm just a female
nothing
and no prize.

Bones on the floor
a dry dust girl
Basquiat teeth
elbows out
swinging an ax
above my head.
No one says look
at that old white woman
they don't say look
at all–
but, they should. I do have
an ax that shrieks on
the down stroke
and pulls
with a negative suck
on the back stroke.

Autopsy for a Martyr

I had to step out of the room after I made that first cut
when light poured out of your chest.
Just exactly who had been murdered here?
They brought you, gunshot, from the ER just after midnight
under a full moon.
Now a super moon is shining from the interior of your body.
My assistant says *retract his ribs*
expose the entire thorax.
Everything is glowing in there.
Out here where we live, we try not to shine.

My Horse Blueway

I take the metal bit out of his soft mouth.
Who can live with a piece of steel across his tongue?
Blueway places his horse forehead against mine, so gentle
telling me go ahead I'll take you anywhere.
He leans down. I step onto his muscular neck. He lifts me
into the saddle fabricated from memory foam
covered in micro fiber soft as suede, it cushions
my bones, as I begin a last journey.

Despite Planet Fitness
there is a *panniculus,*
a hanging flap of stomach
that rests lightly on my lap.
an adolescent girl lives under it
in my vagina who might sing
if I speak to her in
a wordless language.

My "visit from the goon squad"
dissolves into miniscule fragments
mixes with the light of the moon
dances into orbit–
A dolly with a hole in her stocking
Transient Ischemic Attack
breaks the brain like a sudden
barrage of decibels,
leaving a cardboard sign that says
VACANCY Nobody home Out to Lunch
the note I left an indecipherable scribble.
Although I have been many competent
things, I will be, in the words of the EMT,
an elderly female, no radial pulse–
a Mrs. clutching her emergency papers,
wishing for my favorite horse.

Immutable

Too young to be labeled "Greatest"
too old to be a Baby Boomer,

I'm of the unlabeled generation
not tagged by the youngers

in their obsessive indicating.
Too invisible for them to think up a special

term, like "Gen Old." What good luck.
I do get "Honey" and "Sweetie"

in a checkout line or restaurant
and "Perfect!" when I manage

to order food. My snakes have
stopped behaving like clocks

have wrapped around my wrists giving
me the wisdom that comes through

knowing the difference between what
seems unchangeable and what is permanent.

Acknowledgments

"Questions for the Defendant (Accusations)" appeared in the *North of Oxford Anthology: Pandemic of Violence* Winter 2021.

"Studio Trees" appeared in *Ovunque Siamo* 2021

"Art in the Time of Savages" nominated for a Pushcart Prize, appeared in *Ovunque Siamo* 2018. It is the inspiration for an array of prints represented by Raven Fine Arts Editions.

"Trans-specied" nominated for a Pushcart Prize, appeared in *Stillwater Review* 2017.

Thanks to Jennifer Egan for her title *A Visit from the Goon Squad* in reference to aging that I used in the poem "My Horse Blueway."

Gratitude to the A.V. Christie Chapbook contest for reading a shorter form of this manuscript and informing me it made the top ten.

Gratitude also for David Wojahn telling me that I should not abandon narrative.

A thank you to Grace Cavalieri for reminding me that courage is a partner in writing poetry.

Great gratitude to J. C. Todd for her workshop on Resonance in Poems and to Vernita Hall for reading this collection and inspiring some of the poetry in it.

A grateful heart to Cathleen Cohen for writing about the collection and her astute observations.

A heartfelt thank you to Curlee Raven Holton of Raven Studio for reading and commenting, and for many years of conversation and art making.

About the Author

MaryAnn L. Miller is the author of *Falling into the Diaspora* (Finishing Line Press 2023), *Cures for Hysteria* (Finishing Line Press 2018) and *Locus Mentis* (PS Books 2012.) She has been thrice nominated for a Pushcart Prize. Her poetry, book reviews or essays have appeared, among others, in *Mom Egg Review, Wild River Review, Presence Journal, Ovanque Siamo, Stillwater Review, Wordgathering, Kaleidoscope, Passager, Journal of NJ Poets, The International Review of African America Art*, and the anthologies *Illness as a Form of Existence, The Pandemic of Violence,* and *Welcome to the Resistance.*

A visual artist, Miller's artist books are in the collections of the National Museum of Women in the Arts, Stanford University, Bieneke Library at Yale and many others. Miller was the founder and publisher of Lucia Press collaborating with artists and poets. Miller was the Resident Book Artist in the Experimental Printmaking Institute at Lafayette College for sixteen years. She has taught art and reading to middle schoolers, and been a School Counselor to grades Kindergarten to Eight in NJ Public Schools. She has had the rare disease Hyperkalemic Periodic Paralysis since she was three years old. www.maryannlmiller.com

Made in the USA
Middletown, DE
11 February 2024